HEIRS OF THE
ANCIENT MAYA

HEIRS OF TH

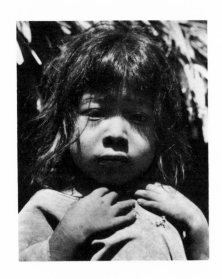

ANCIENT MAYA

A Portrait of the Lacandon Indians

by **CHRISTINE PRICE**

Photographs by

GERTRUDE DUBY BLOM

CHARLES SCRIBNER'S SONS · NEW YORK

For Old Chank'in
and the people of Nahá

Printed in the United States of America
Library of Congress Catalog Card Number 78-37191
SBN 684-12811-X (trade cloth, RB)

CONTENTS

Author's Note   6

1 THE SONG OF THE JAGUAR   8

2 THE WAY OF THE PEOPLE   22

3 THE WAY OF THE GODS   38

4 THE GIFT OF THE SINGING GOD   52

author's note

I first met Gertrude Duby Blom in the winter of 1970. On a journey in Mexico, I had come to stay for a few days at Mrs. Blom's beautiful house in San Cristóbal de Las Casas in the highlands of Chiapas. It was then that I saw her photographs of the Lacandon Indians.

Those pictures—hundreds of them—were the fruit of many years of friendship and a deep love for the Lacandons. With her husband, the late Dr. Frans Blom, Mrs. Blom had made long and difficult expeditions into the Lacandon forest, not only to meet the Indians but to explore and map the ruined temples of their ancestors, the ancient Maya. She always carried her camera to record the portraits of the Lacandons, their way of living and the beauty of their land.

Today, Mrs. Blom makes frequent visits to her Lacandon friends. I am very grateful to her for taking me to meet them at Nahá, and for all her help and encouragement during the making of this book.

I would also like to thank Miss Jeannette Mirsky and Mr. Frank Waters for reading my manuscript and giving me helpful suggestions.

I am grateful to Praeger Publishers, Inc., New York, and to Thames and Hudson Ltd., London, for their kind permission to include the poem on page 52, quoted from *The Maya* by Michael D. Coe.

Finally I want to thank the people of Nahá, who accepted me as a friend of their beloved Gertrudis. This is their book.

C. P.

HEIRS OF THE
ANCIENT MAYA

1 THE SONG OF
THE JAGUAR

"Your voice comes from far, from far away.
I hear your voice.
It comes from a great hill. . . ."

Old Chank'in, the Lacandon Indian, is singing the Song of the Jaguar. The low notes of his chanting drift along the narrow trail under the trees—mighty mahogany and sapodilla and the sacred ceiba tree, its trunk ghost-pale against the green.

Here in the heart of the Lacandon forest we are in a world of greenness. A cloak of rich green growth covers all things, smothering the works of nature and of man, last year's fallen tree trunks and the stone-carved records of men who lived here more than a thousand years ago.

In the green twilight, past, present, and future are mingled in one flow of time, measured by sunrise and sunset, the waxing and waning of the moon, the seasonal movements of the planets. Here the past still lives. A glimpse of old stonework, half-hidden

Ceiba tree in the Lacandon forest. The ancient Maya believed the ceiba was the first tree, the ancestor of all life.

*Carved
inscription
in hieroglyphs,
the writing of
the ancient Maya*

among the leaves, or a silent deserted building overgrown with ferns and orchids can draw us backward through the flow of time. Even the simple words of Chank'in's song are echoes of the past.

"Your voice comes from far, from far away. . . ."

The language of the Jaguar Song is the common speech of Old Chank'in and his people, the Maya language of their ancestors. The Lacandon Indians have a proud heritage. They are linked across the centuries with one of the greatest civilizations of ancient America. They are heirs of the ancient Maya.

A thousand years before Columbus came to the New World, the Lacandon forest and the vast lowland forest of Guatemala were the heartland of the Maya. Between A.D. 300 and 900 the Maya cities rose proud and white, like islands in the sea of green. The forest was patched with corn fields and villages, and criss-crossed by a network of trails that were alive with people— farmers and traders, princes and priests.

Ruins of a Maya temple near the Lacandon settlement at Lacanhá

The men of those days lived in simple wooden houses, roofed with thatch, as the Lacandons do today; but the Maya gods were given houses of stone, made beautiful with sculptures and paintings. The Maya cities were cities of temples, ceremonial centers dedicated to the worship of the gods. Standing stones, tall and richly carved, were set up in the temple plazas to mark the passing of time. The men who carved these stelae with hieroglyphic writing and noble human figures were directed in their work by the priests, who were all-powerful in the eyes of the people.

The Maya priests had devised a wonderful calendar for the measurement of time, reaching deep into the past and far ahead into the future. To the Maya, time was holy. The days themselves were gods, both good and evil.

When the priests consulted the calendar and proclaimed a time of worship and sacrifice, the people flocked to the temple cities. There they watched in awe as the priests moved slowly up the steps of the temples—fantastic figures plumed with the long green tail feathers of the sacred quetzal bird and loaded with ornaments of holy jade.

Only the priests knew how to seek the favor of the gods and to pray for good crops of corn that the people might have food. Even the jaguar of Chank'in's song was worshiped as a god by the ancient Maya. The priests who served him were clothed in spotted jaguar skins. When they came forth to burn incense and offer sacrifice, musicians would blow on long trumpets, shake the rattles and beat the drums, and singers would raise their voices in a ritual chant.

Today the plumed priests and crowds of worshipers are gone and the temple cities are crumbling ruins, but in the shadow

This richly dressed Maya priest, with his two attendants, is carved on a stela at Bonampak. The steps behind the stela lead up from the plaza to the temples on the high acropolis.

12

Carved lintel from a doorway in the great temple city of Yaxchilán. The figure on the right holds the head of a jaguar.

of the trees we can still hear the low voice of Old Chank'in singing the Song of the Jaguar, the lord of the forest. The hypnotic chanting binds the listeners like a spell. In the last words it is the jaguar himself who speaks:

"I am weary.
I seek a fallen tree to enter in and sleep.
My tail waves and I lift my feet.
I have a spotted skin.
The wind is in my ears. . . ."

Now the song is ended, and Chank'in and his companions, sitting beside the forest trail, talk together in the language of their ancestors. Their hair hangs loose about their faces and they wear the simple cotton tunics that were the dress of Maya Indians before the Spanish conquest. But how are they linked

14

with the temples, the Jaguar Priests, and the glorious sculptures hidden in the forest?

There are mysteries in the story of the Lacandons, as in the history of the ancient Maya. Scholars have learned much about the Maya through the excavation of the ruined temple cities. They have read names and dates and astronomical records in the Maya hieroglyphic writing. But much will remain hidden until the writing has been fully deciphered and more of the stone-carved inscriptions can be understood.

Tracing the origin of the Lacandons leads us into the darkest of the Maya mysteries—the collapse of the great culture in the forest six hundred years before the Spaniards conquered Mexico. The discoveries of archaeologists have shown that in the

Old Chank'in and two of the young men of Nahá

ninth century the building of temples and carving of stelae suddenly came to an end. The reason is still unknown.

Perhaps the soil was exhausted and the corn crops failed, so that the Maya had to move away or starve. Perhaps the people rebelled against their rulers or suffered the attacks of warlike tribes from the north. Whatever the cause—or combination of causes—the cities were deserted by the priests and rulers of the people. By the tenth century the center of Maya power had shifted to the dry hot land of northern Yucatán, already the home of men of Maya stock.

Yet scattered groups of people probably remained behind in the forest after their leaders had gone. Some scholars believe that these were the ancestors of the Lacandons. Others suggest that because their language is akin to the Maya speech of Yucatán the Lacandons must have traveled south from the Yucatán peninsula to settle in the great forest, some time before the coming of the Spaniards.

When Cortez and his conquistadors invaded Mexico in the sixteenth century, the days of Maya greatness were past, but Indians speaking Maya languages were widely spread over southern Mexico and Central America, as they still are today. They were proud people and they put up a desperate resistance against the Spanish invaders. In Yucatán, above all, there were years of hard fighting before the Maya were subdued and had accepted the Christian faith of the conquerors. Only the Lacandons refused to submit.

The Lacandons earned the reputation of a fierce and warlike tribe. Again and again they threw back the Spanish expeditions that invaded the forest. They chose death rather than slavery under the rule of the conquistadors. Stories of battles against the Spaniards became legends among the Lacandons, who never forgot the coming of the terrible "Thunderbolts," the bearded white men with guns. Yet the spirit of the Lacandons could not be broken, either by the guns of the "Thunderbolts" or by the

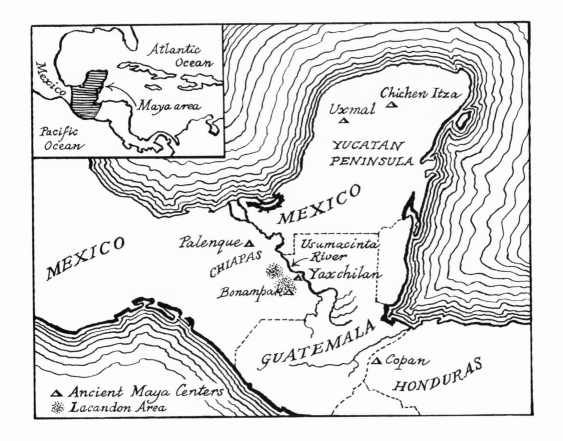

preaching of the brave Spanish friars who strove to convert the Indians to Christianity.

Map of the Maya area

At last the Lacandons were left alone to follow in the ways of their fathers.

For many years they lived at peace, farming, fishing, and hunting in their good land of forest and winding rivers and calm blue lakes. They were a Stone Age people, almost unknown to the rest of the world. After the Spanish attacks on their villages, they gave up village life and settled in small family groups, hidden deep in the forest. They built no temples and they lost the ancient Maya knowledge of mathematics and writing, but they still paid homage to the old holy places. They burned incense before the weatherworn sculptures and prayed to the gods of their ancestors. Old religious beliefs, held in the memories of

17

Old Chank'in

the wise men of the people, were faithfully passed down from father to son.

Old Chank'in received the ancient wisdom from his father, and it is his task to teach the young men and boys. His father taught him the Jaguar Song, and Chank'in explains to us its meaning.

The song has the power to protect a man from jaguars. A

hunter may be quite alone in the forest at night, but if he sings this song, the jaguars will listen and go away to sleep in a distant place and leave the man unharmed.

"For in my father's time," says Old Chank'in, "there were many, many *tigres* in the mountains."

Today there are few jaguars left in the forest, and within the lifetime of Old Chank'in great changes have come to the green world of the Lacandons. Outsiders have invaded their land—a peaceful invasion but terrible in its effect.

The first to come were the mahogany-cutters at the turn of the century. When they met the Indians, the white men called them *Caribes*, a name which the Lacandons still use when talking in Spanish with outsiders. The Caribes proved very helpful to the lumbermen. There were no big stands of mahogany in the forest, and finding the trees meant hacking trails through thick undergrowth. The Indians often served as guides, and the lumbermen rewarded them with white men's goods.

The Lacandons gladly gave up their old bows and arrows and stone knives for shotguns and keen steel machetes, but they also received the white men's cheap liquor and deadly diseases. Scores of Indians died of sickness they could not cure or resist.

Then, in the years of the Second World War, men came to the forest to gather chicle, the rubbery sap of the sapodilla tree, for making chewing gum. Small bands of *chicleros* would set out from their big central camps to find the sapodilla, or chicozapote, as they called it. Again the Lacandons were guides. The Indians also brought their fruit and vegetables and tobacco to trade in the chicle camps for the wonderful goods of the white men.

The chicleros thought nothing of cheating the Indians or simply stealing what they wanted. The Lacandons would not steal. Although they learned, through hard experience, to hate the chicleros, they continued to trade with them for cotton cloth, ammunition, salt, and bad liquor.

But still the Indians were dying from the diseases brought

19

*Ancient Maya
sculpture from
Palenque, Chiapas*

in by the invaders, and whole settlements in the forest were deserted. Today the Lacandons, who once were many, number less than three hundred people. All of them, except for a handful in Guatemala, live in the State of Chiapas, on the Mexican side of the great Usumacinta River.

The people are split into two groups, separated by many miles of forest. Chank'in's people belong to the northern group, which is scattered over a broad stretch of land with its biggest settlement on the shore of Lake Nahá. The Lacandons to the south are clustered about the village of Lacanhá, on the banks of the Lacanhá River. The two groups do not mix with each other; they even have different customs, dress, and dialect.

At Lacanhá the people have been more influenced by outsiders. Much of their old religion has been forgotten, for the elders of the village, who served as priests, have died without passing on their knowledge. Missionaries have come to Lacanhá, and most of the people have adopted Christian beliefs.

The Lacandons of Nahá, led by Old Chank'in, have resisted change. They have clung to the old traditions, deep-rooted in the past. Yet change has been forced upon them. They have accepted the goods of the white man, even while they suffered from his invasion of their land.

20

Many centuries lie between the people of Nahá and the Maya of the mighty temple cities. Much has happened to alter old ways of life and work and worship. Do these Lacandons still follow the ways of their ancestors? They may be heirs of the ancient Maya, but without the temples and the learned priests how much of the old heritage lives on?

Chanbor,
a man of Nahá

If anyone can reveal to us the true answers, it is Old Chank'in. As he rises to take the trail back to his house on the far side of Lake Nahá, his last word to us is an invitation to meet him again soon. *"Saman!"* he says. *"Tomorrow!"*

The young men and boys get up to follow him home, and suddenly, in the forest twilight, their faces become the carved profiles on an ancient stela. Then they vanish into the green world of the trees, the shadowy kingdom of the jaguar.

21

2 THE WAY OF
THE PEOPLE

A new day comes to the forest, and white mist rises from the still water of Lake Nahá. In the cool half-light of dawn, dew has fallen on the leaves like gentle rain, and now the world is refreshed. Tiny hummingbirds go whirring and buzzing in the underbrush along the forest fringe, and out in the lake the water lilies spread their petals to the sun.

A long dugout canoe, newly cut from a giant mahogany tree, lies at the water's edge, and two of the young men of Nahá are waiting to take us across the lake.

We sit down comfortably on the flat bottom of the canoe. The new wood has the pinkish hue of good mahogany, and the high straight sides are neatly cut. The ancient Maya would not have scorned the workmanship of the men of Nahá.

The canoe glides silently away with easy strokes of the long paddles, and the ripples of our passing stir the reflections of the deep green trees along the wooded shore.

K'in, paddling in the bow, tells how the men and boys of the lake settlement worked together to make the canoe. After they had felled the chosen tree in the forest, they spent five days

Making the dugout canoe in the forest

carving out a section of the trunk with ax, adze, and machete. They took another day to haul the canoe down to the lake and to launch it from the low-lying shore where we come in to land this morning. Small tree trunks were laid in the wet mud to make a causeway for dragging the canoe to the water, and we follow the causeway through the bushes to the settlement.

The little group of thatched houses, set among vegetable gardens and old corn patches, is quiet in the morning sun. Dogs

are dozing on the dusty earth and chickens scratch under the orange trees. Old Chank'in and some of the others have already gone into the forest to clear a new *milpa* for corn planting, and the women are busy indoors.

Several families live together here, but often a Lacandon will build his family house and compound, called a *caribal*, far from any neighbors. If his friends want to visit him, they must announce their coming by a shout or a whistle outside the caribal. The old custom was for visitors to arrive unarmed, having left their weapons beside the trail, as a sign of friendship.

Here at Nahá the people already know we are coming, but there are still formalities to be observed.

Palm-thatched houses with cleared land in front and the forest behind

25

Before entering a house we must ask: "*Taringrech*? May I come in?"

"*Or ken*. Come in," is the answer, and then: "*Kulen*. Sit down."

The houses are cool and shadowy inside, for there are no windows. Sunlight slants through the doorway and filters between the upright wooden slats of the walls, falling in stripes on the earth floor. A fire smolders in the middle of the room, and from the smoke-blackened roof beams hang bags of vegetables, leaf-wrapped packages of salt, dried gourds, and bundles of home-grown tobacco.

String hammocks and low wooden beds serve for sleeping at night and resting in the daytime, and there may be bowls of gray wood-ashes under the beds, placed there the night before for a little extra warmth.

The woman of the house sits cross-legged by the hearth where she does the cooking. Corn simmers over the fire in an iron pot, ready for making the corn dough called *posol*. Rolled into balls and wrapped in banana leaves, posol is always at hand for use when needed. Meals come at irregular times and people eat when they are hungry, but no meal is complete without corn.

Posol can be mixed with water and flavored with chili pepper, cacao, or wild honey, and it is good food to take on a hunting trip or for a day's work in the milpa. Later in the day the women will be making big flat tortillas, patted into shape on a low table and quickly cooked in a shallow earthenware dish propped on the hearthstones. Tortillas are the bread of central Mexico and were unknown to the ancient Maya. They used to make their corn into tamales, as the Lacandons often do. Tamales, stuffed with meat or beans and boiled in a wrapping of leaves, make a good evening meal.

If the man of the house has two, or even three, wives, each one will tend her own fire and cook for her own children. The youngest wife may be no more than a child herself, and the eldest, who rules the household, is like a grandmother to her.

In the past the people were divided into many clans, named after animals such as the spider monkey or the peccary. Members of the same clan were closely related, and a man had to find a wife outside his clan. Now that the people are so few they no longer keep to this rule nor follow the old strict pattern for naming their children.

A firstborn son always had to be called K'in, meaning "Sun," and a first daughter, Nak'in, "Sun of the House." The

This mother carries her baby in a net bag, supported by the tumpline around her head, while she prepares the food for her family. At the left is her new metal mill for grinding corn.

second son was K'ayyum, named after the Lacandons' god of song, and the third one was Chank'in, "Little Sun."

The girls of the family must be prepared for early marriage, and they soon learn to help with housework and cooking and to look after chickens, pet dogs and cats. Lacandon children are not often scolded, and the smallest ones are carried about by their mothers everywhere—down to the lake for water, or out to the vegetable gardens and fruit trees.

A baby rides on his mother's back when she goes from the house to the little thatched shed where food is made ready for cooking. Here the corn is softened by soaking it with lime made from crushed snail shells from the lake; and here too, in the old days, the corn was ground on the heavy stone *metate*. Now the

Cloth can be made from mahagua bark by beating it for many hours until it is thin and supple. Headbands of bark cloth, dyed red, are worn in religious ceremonies.

The loom for weaving cotton cloth is fastened to a tree or a post and held taut by the strap around the weaver's waist. This weaver, like all married women of Nahá, wears yellow parrot feathers on her long braid.

Baskets are woven of tough vines.

women of Nahá have new metal corn mills to make their work easier, and they prefer new pans and basins of bright enamel to the old homemade clay cooking pots.

The Lacandons are not as self-sufficient as their ancestors were. Many things they need and want must come from a world that most of them have never seen. The white cotton cloth for tunics and the gay red prints for women's skirts are brought from markets far beyond the forest, either by the Indians themselves or by traveling peddlers.

The people still grow a little cotton, and a few of the women have back-strap looms for weaving cloth, usually for the tunics worn by their husbands in religious ceremonies. The natural riches of the forest, too, can be made into many useful and beautiful things—a basket, a strongly knotted hammock or a

31

*The wife of
Mateo of Nahá
makes a
clay doll.*

carrying bag. A woman may model sticky brown clay into a doll
for a child, but the making of clay pots is men's work, along
with housebuilding and farming the land. The men love to hunt
and fish, and their wives will sometimes go with them far into
the forest to gather wild fruit or to find the nests of honeybees.

Today Old Chank'in has taken his three wives with him to
the milpa, and K'in, who paddled us across the lake, will guide
us through the forest to find them.

We take a narrow trail past the vegetable gardens where the
people grow sweet potatoes, onions, pineapples, watermelons,
and sugarcane. There are long-stemmed papaya trees and clumps

of banana with bright green shiny leaves; and K'in points out a jicara tree, loaded with its queer round fruit. When the jicaras are ripe to be picked, cleaned out and dried, they will be used as ceremonial drinking bowls at the god-house.

Past the jicara tree the path threads through a thicket of underbrush on the edge of the forest, land that was once cleared and planted and now lies fallow. The Lacandons follow the old way of "slash and burn" farming, like the ancient Maya before them. When a man has chosen a patch of forest as the place for his new milpa, he cuts down the trees during the dry season and burns the branches and brush. In April, just before the coming of the summer rains, the forest is veiled in the smoke from burning milpas. Then the corn is planted, along with squash and beans, between the half-burned tree trunks.

The Lacandon farmer does his planting with a digging stick, as his ancestors did, prodding holes in the soil for the precious seeds. He weeds his field twice in the rainy growing time, and the corn is harvested between August and October. After three or four harvests the earth will no longer give a good crop of corn; then it is time to choose a place for a new milpa.

In the Lacandon forest pines are often the first trees to take root in an old corn field. Many pines grow on the high ridges of the rugged hills; their seeds are easily carried to the lower slopes by birds or by the wind. The young pine trees spring up quickly in the poor soil of the milpa, and under their shadow the seedlings of hardwood trees begin to grow. When the short-lived pines have died and rotted away, the hardwoods will stand tall and beautiful and their falling leaves will enrich the soil.

Deep in the earth of the Guatemalan forest are the remains of pine trees that grew there on abandoned fields of the ancient Maya, a thousand years ago. Perhaps this gives a clue to the mystery of the Maya—the reason for the collapse of their civilization in the forest. The Maya cities and the farming settlements that surrounded them had populations of many hundreds of people. Were there at last more people than the forest could sustain?

Even the Lacandons, so few in number, need plenty of space for their "slash and burn" farming, and around their caribals little game is left for the hunters, except parrots and monkeys. K'in says they must travel far to find wild pig and deer.

There is still no sign of Chank'in's milpa, but as we follow K'in up the steep wooded hill, we pass the mahogany tree that was cut down to make the canoe. The head and butt of the mighty trunk lie where they fell. The long gap between them, where the canoe was cut out and hollowed, is thickly carpeted with slices of pink, sweet-smelling wood, as big as roof shingles.

K'ayyum's small brother helps to clear the milpa.

Then, out of the twilight of the forest, we come to an open place, flooded with hot sunshine. The dark soil lies bare between the weathered gray trunks of felled trees, and green plants of tobacco are sprouting. This is an important crop for the Lacandons, who love to smoke enormous homemade cigars and can also sell their bundles of tobacco to traders. Sprawling tomato plants with tiny white flowers are set about amongst the tobacco, and ears of corn from last year's harvest are neatly stacked in a little thatched hut close by.

At last we come to the new milpa—a field of naked brown earth and tree stumps backed by a wooded hillside that rings with the *chock-chock* of swinging machetes. While we watch, a tall tree on the edge of the wood sways, leans, and falls with a crash onto the mass of tree trunks and green branches below.

A slab of mahogany from the canoe tree is made into a table. Young Chank'in uses his machete to carve out the top and the short legs in one piece.

35

At the foot of the hill Old Chank'in is at work with his three wives, tearing strips of bark from some felled mahagua trees. After long soaking in the lake, the bark will yield tough fibers for making nets and string hammocks. The youngest wife carries her baby on her back, and all three women swing their machetes with the skill and strength of men, chopping through the bark and prying it off the tree trunks.

Trees are still crashing down higher up the hill, and there we find twelve-year-old K'ayyum and his small brother, wielding machetes almost as long as themselves and bringing down the tall slender trees exactly as they wish them to fall. They are learning men's work in the only school they know, a school where living and learning are one, and where life may depend on the skill of the hand, the sharpness of eye and ear.

K'ayyum is a gifted boy and a quick learner, and he will soon have all the knowledge he needs to make a living, following the way of his people. But a man must know more than that. Above and beyond the way of the people is the way of the gods.

Under the guidance of his father, Old Chank'in, K'ayyum has already begun to take part in the ceremonies at the god-house in the lakeside settlement. Women are not allowed in the god-house; only men and boys may go there to burn the copal incense and chant the ceremonial songs.

Another tree crashes to the earth, and Chank'in smiles as the work goes on. His eldest wife, thin and small, passes by with a heavy load of bark strips, bound for the lake, her brown feet making no sound on the bare soil.

The way of the people is a simple way, fitted to the world they live in. The way of the gods is full of strangeness and wonder and the mystery of ancient things half-understood. Yet the unseen gods govern the life and work of the people, as they ruled the lives of the Maya long ago.

No corn can be planted here in the milpa without prayer and sacrifice; when the harvest is gathered, the gods must be given the first fruits before the people may eat. Nothing will grow from the earth without the good will of the gods, for theirs were the hands that created the world and the living things that dwell in it—the Indian, the white man, and all the beasts and birds and plants. The way of the gods leads back to the beginning of all things, when the world was made and men first walked the earth. . . .

K'ayyum,
son of
Old Chank'in

37

3 THE WAY OF
THE GODS

"Hachakyum is good, he is always good. He made the world, the trees, the hills, the milpa, the tobacco, the tigre and all the other animals that are here. And he made men out of clay. He made us, the Caribes. . . ."

When Old Chank'in tells of the gods, the words come singing to his lips. He speaks with excited gestures of his hands, and his eyes are alight with joy.

We are sitting with him in the sunshine outside the god-house, a little way up the slope from the settlement. The god-house is an open building, without walls, its thatched roof set on stout posts. In the shadows under the roof we can see the rows of pottery incense burners—"god-pots"—neatly arranged on shelves, and on the floor below are large jicaras filled with copal, the incense of the ancient Maya. Other things needed for ceremonies are stowed among the beams—bark-cloth headbands, strips of dried bark for making *balché*, the ceremonial drink, and a net bag full of jicara drinking bowls.

Two god-pots stand in the middle of the floor where Chank'in and his old friend Mateo burned incense this morning, chanting prayers while they fed the fires in the pots.

Old Chank'in and K'in outside the god-house

"And where did all the gods come from, Chank'in?" we ask. Each of the pots in the god-house represents a god, and there are many.

"K'akoch made Hachakyum, and then he made many flowers. The other gods were born from the flowers."

There is no god-pot for the distant shadowy K'akoch, for no one prays to him. Hachakyum is the chief of the gods and the ruler of the world.

"Hachakyum made the Caribes," says Old Chank'in, "but he did not make the white people."

"Who made them?"

"Akyantho made them. And he made the machete and the shotgun and the horse and all the other things that are not here, the things that belong to the white men. Akyantho is the brother of Hachakyum."

The chief god has another brother too—Sukunkyum, who is the judge of people's souls when they die. He lives in the underworld and he is stern and just. Good people may go to heaven, but the souls of bad people are turned into animals by the evil god, Kisin, and forced to serve him in the underworld. When Kisin is angry, he shakes the posts of his house until the whole earth trembles.

Sukunkyum fights against Kisin to protect the souls of the people and also to help the sun. The Lacandons believe, as their ancestors did, that the sun goes down into the underworld each night. As he travels the long dark road beneath the earth, the sun must wrestle with Kisin and defeat him before the dawn of a new day.

Hachakyum watches over the earth at night, passing along the Milky Way, his trail across the sky. The many little stars, too small to name, are his seeds of corn and beans and squash and all the other vegetables, and the moon is his wife, Okna.

"I shall pray to Okna," says Chank'in, "when my wife is going to have a baby. I shall pray that all will be well."

Chank'in shares the god-house with his neighbors, Mateo and Antonio. Each man, as head of his family, keeps his own pots in the god-house and may go there at any time to burn incense and chant prayers for the birth of a child, for safety on a journey, or for good health.

Chank'in explains that pains and fevers are sent to people by Mensabak, the god of rain and thunder, or by K'ak, the fire god, but never by Hachakyum.

When Chank'in performs a curing ceremony for someone who is sick, he makes little green wands of palm leaf. Chanting in a low monotone, he blackens the leaves in the smoke of incense from the god-pot, then lightly touches them to the body of the one who is ill or in pain.

Praying in the god-house while copal incense burns in the pots

*The men and
boys of Nahá
drink balché
after offering
it to the gods.*

Among the many ceremonies at the god-house the greatest
comes in spring before the planting of the corn. The ancient
Maya worshiped a corn god, young and beautiful, and the farmers looked to the priests to tell them when to plant the corn.
The Lacandons have no priests to guide them in their work and
worship, but the older men, like Old Chank'in, still have some
knowledge of the stars and of the ancient calendar. They too
have a god, Ak'inchob, who is lord of the milpa and the corn,
and for them, as for their ancestors, the planting of the corn is
a holy act. Before he goes to the milpa with his digging stick
and seeds a man must be purified in body and soul.

The great spring ceremony lasts fifteen days with all the
people of the settlement gathering at the god-house. The women
make posol and tamales to be offered to the gods, and balché is

42

prepared by mixing the bark of the balché tree with water and sugarcane and letting it ferment in the long wooden trough outside the god-house. Balché is a holy drink, belonging to the ancient tradition. The Lacandons say it was created by the sun and moon and has the power to wash away all evil.

"When we drink the balché," says Old Chank'in, "we drink the sun and moon."

Spring is also the season for making new god-pots and renewing the equipment in the god-house. The head of each family makes his own set of pots from clay, always in the same shape, with the head of the god roughly modeled on one side. He paints the pots with white lime, charcoal, and a red paint made from the berries of the achiote tree. The new pots are consecrated by a long ritual in the god-house. Sacred stones are removed from the old pots and put into the new ones. The gods then come to live in the new vessels, and the old empty pots are carried away and left in hidden caves.

But the gods can live in many places at once. Caves and lakes, deep in the forest, are hallowed by their presence, and men may go there to worship and to pray. Ts'ibatnah, the god of writing and painting, lives at the beautiful lake, Itzanoku, where there are strange rock-pictures, painted by unknown hands. K'ak and Mensabak also have lakes of their own.

"And where does Hachakyum live?" we ask.

Chank'in points east toward the Usumacinta River beyond the horizon. "Hachakyum lives there. His house is at Yaxchilán."

Yaxchilán! The glory of the past is in that name. Yaxchilán is one of the great Maya ruins on the banks of the Usumacinta. . . .

"And are there other places where the gods live?"

"They live at Bonampak and Palenque."

Once more Chank'in speaks the names of ancient cities. Bonampak, with its famous painted walls, is in the midst of the forest, a short distance from Lacanhá; but Palenque, perhaps the loveliest of Maya ruins, is far away at the forest's edge.

43

The air is always soft and moist at Palenque, and the gray stonework of the buildings is clothed in lush green moss and orange lichen. Bunches of ferns spill out of crevices in the walls; and three small temples, set against the dark curtain of the forest, are perched on mounds like gardens, carpeted in spring with wild begonias.

The Palace at Palenque with its watchtower and many rooms and patios

Chank'in has never traveled to Palenque, has never seen the palace and the temples rising like ghosts in the swirl of morning mist. Yet he speaks of Palenque as the holiest place of all, the center of the world. In the sky above the temples is the heart of heaven, the true home of Hachakyum, and in the earth beneath is the heart of the underworld, the realm of Sukunkyum. Palenque was the birthplace of all the gods, and the first men were made there, together with the holy corn that was to be their food.

It is said that the Lacandons knew of the ancient tomb at Palenque, deep in the stone pyramid of the Temple of Inscriptions, long before the tomb was discovered by archaeologists. A great Maya ruler was buried under the temple thirteen centuries ago. His tall body, with the face masked in jade mosaic,

Opposite:
The Temple of the Foliated Cross, named for its relief carving of a cross adorned with corn leaves

45

The Temple of Inscriptions at Palenque

was laid in a massive stone coffin that was decorated with exquisite carvings in relief.

The sculptors of Palenque, working in stone or hard white stucco, made relief carving into a glorious art. The roofs and walls of the buildings were covered with carved decoration as rich and complicated as the dense leafage of the forest.

The decorations of the temples reveal the symbols of heaven and earth and underworld and of the multitudinous

Maya gods, the snarling mask of the jaguar and the gentle face of the young corn god emerging from the leaves of growing corn. The Lacandons say that of all the company of gods at Palenque it was Ak'inchob, the corn god, who was summoned by Hachakyum to undertake a great and difficult task. He was to build a new city for the gods to dwell in. That city was Yaxchilán.

Who can blame the Lacandons for saying that Yaxchilán was built by a god? How could the hands of men, using only the stone tools of the Maya, quarry and shape the colossal building stones and rear the temples, beautiful even in their ruin?

Portrait of a warrior on a great stela at Bonampak

Old Chank'in and his son approach the headless statue in the doorway of the house of Hachakyum at Yaxchilán.

In the time of the ancient Maya, Yaxchilán was a powerful city, dominating the smaller center at Bonampak. There were not only hundreds of men to toil at the priests' command on the never-ending task of building and enlarging the temples. There were skilled sculptors to carve the stone lintels over the doorways and to adorn the plazas with magnificent stelae.

Perhaps the same artists also worked at Bonampak, where the relief carvings are equally fine. Bonampak, with its small temples on a high green acropolis, is a peaceful place today, but in the past it must have known strife and even invasion. Its art speaks of war. The greatest stela shows the brilliant portrait of a warrior lord, and the murals of the famous painted building tell the story of a battle. Maya leaders make ready for war, lead out their men to vanquish the enemy, and celebrate the victory with music and dance.

Only a strong fierce god should dwell in such a place, and the Lacandons used to say that Bonampak was the home of U Hachil, the guardian of the forest and of poisonous snakes. U Hachil was the brother-in-law of Hachakyum, the true lord and ruler of the world.

Old Chank'in speaks in awe of Yaxchilán and the house of Hachakyum. His people used to go on pilgrimages to the ancient city; and a few years back Chank'in walked there from Nahá with one of his sons, bringing copal to offer to Hachakyum.

The two men passed quietly among the ruins, where hundreds of worshipers had gathered long ago to watch the Maya priests make sacrifice to the gods. Now the greenness of the forest had crept over temples and plazas. The stonework was gripped by the roots of trees, and only a long-tailed macaw flew off with a flash of scarlet as the Lacandons went by.

At last they drew near to the temple that is the house of Hachakyum.

The high god dwells in a headless statue seated in a doorway. The head, broken off by mahogany-cutters many years ago, lies on the ground. The breaking of the statue gave rise to a new belief among the Lacandons. They say that when the head is reunited with the statue, the end of the world will come and

*The headless
statue at
Yaxchilán*

jaguars will descend upon the earth to devour the people. Only
the Lacandons know how to pray to Hachakyum to spare the
world from destruction.

Today, as we rise to leave the god-house, the end of the
world seems very far away. The little settlement is quiet and
peaceful in the drowsy heat of noon. Chank'in's eldest wife is
sitting outside the house with her sewing, and young K'ayyum
is busy making jaguars out of clay. In his clever hands the shape-
less lumps of clay are formed into fierce snarling animals. When
they are dry and hard, he will paint their spotted skins in white,
black, and yellow.

Old Chank'in joins us, his face crinkled in a smile, and a
ripple of laughter comes from the little group of men in the shade

of an orange tree. One of them has made some arrows for us, fine arrows with beautifully shaped flint tips and with parrot feathers fitted at the butt of the shaft. These arrows are good for hunting, he says, and would kill a jaguar or a deer. Not like the poor blunt arrows with gaudy feathers that some men make for sale in towns!

Another man has carved a low table from a single slab of mahogany. He trims the legs with delicate cuts of his machete, still not satisfied that the work is good enough. When we start down toward the lake, they promise to bring to us the arrows and table in the afternoon, and we know they will keep their promise.

We step into the canoe that waits beside the muddy shore, and the young men take up the paddles and push off. Out in the still center of the lake we all slip over the side of the boat into the water. The Lacandons swim like fish, their long hair streaming out behind them.

Today the gods are kind. Life is good.

The fallen head of the statue

51

4 THE GIFT OF
THE SINGING GOD

"Eat, eat, thou hast bread;
  Drink, drink, thou hast water;
  On that day, dust possesses the earth;
  On that day, a blight is on the face of the earth,
  On that day, a cloud rises,
  On that day, a mountain rises,
  On that day, a strong man seizes the land,
  On that day, things fall to ruin,
  On that day, the tender leaf is destroyed,
  On that day, the dying eyes are closed. . . .
  And they are scattered afar in the forests."

These words were chanted centuries ago by Chilam Balam, a prophet and priest of the ancient Maya, whose name, Balam, meant "jaguar."

Looking ahead through the flow of time, he prophesied the coming of the Spanish conquistadors and the end of freedom for the Maya people. Long afterward, when the prophecy had been terribly fulfilled, the words of the prophet were set down, in the Maya language but in the writing of the conquerors, in one of

Destruction in the Lacandon forest—the felling of trees

the Books of Chilam Balam, collections of chronicles, prophecies, and myths.

The Maya tribes fought bitterly against the rule of the white men, but only the Lacandons of the great forest were able to preserve their freedom and to follow in their chosen way. Now, in our own century, their way of living and their life as a people have been threatened and almost destroyed. For the Lacandons it has seemed as though the ancient prophecy would once again be fulfilled. "Things fall to ruin . . . the tender leaf is destroyed . . . the dying eyes are closed. . . ."

The contact with white men, after long years of isolation, brought suffering and death to the Lacandons, but their land was little changed by those first invaders. The mahogany-cutters and chicleros took what they wanted from the wealth of the forest and then moved on, leaving their camps and trails to be swallowed up in new green growth. The scars were quickly healed.

But in recent years a new invasion has begun. The Tzeltal Indians have come to the forest, hungry for land. They are a Maya people like the Lacandons, but their ways are more like the ways of the white man. They see the Lacandon forest as a land of rich soil where they can grow good crops and carve out a new life for themselves and their children.

Some of the Tzeltals were formerly landless workers on big plantations along the forest's edge. Others have migrated from distant villages in the highlands of Chiapas, where the hills are gullied with erosion and the soil impoverished. The Tzeltals arrive in the forest as pioneer settlers, brave and hard-working, but with little knowledge of the proper care of the land. Wher-ever they choose to settle, they start work at once to clear away the woods and make room for houses and milpas.

One of the Tzeltal villages is on the Lacandon River, less than an hour's walk from Lake Nahá. A broad trail leads to the village through the forest. In the shade of the trees the muddy earth is churned and pitted by the hoofs of horses and mules and the feet of men who wear shoes.

Bor, the young Lacandon who went with us to the village, picked his way swiftly through the mud on silent bare feet. He slowed down now and then to listen to the rustle of birds in the undergrowth, and once to let a snake wriggle out of our way,

but when we met a stray horse standing in the trail, Bor stopped short. He stood there like one of his ancestors, confronted by a horse of the Spaniards. Then he picked up a stout stick to defend us and skirted warily past the strange beast, eyeing it with distrust.

Bor's people have good reasons to dislike the animals brought into the forest by the Tzeltals, for pigs and mules often stray into the Lacandons' unfenced fields and gardens and destroy the crops. The Tzeltal village, so close to Nahá, is an alien world to the Lacandons. The shelter of the forest has been swept away. The thatched houses are dotted about on a grassy field, short-cropped by cows and horses. The lower slopes of the

Tzeltal settlers on their way to new land in the forest

55

A Tzeltal settlement carved out of the Lacandon forest

wooded hills beyond are strewn with felled trees, and the banks of the Lacandon River, where it flows through the village, are bare of bushes and gouged by the erosion of summer floods.

The Tzeltal village is a small place with few people, but it has changed the face of the forest. It is a warning of things to come and a reminder of things long past.

In the days of the ancient Maya the Lacandon forest supported many hundreds of people. The temple cities of Bonampak and Yaxchilán must have been surrounded by milpas and gardens, and as the soil of the cleared land became exhausted, fresh tracts would be cut over and burned. By the time of the downfall and desertion of the Maya cities, broad stretches of the forest had been cleared and left in a weedy tangle of second growth. It took many years for the forest to recover, and the destruction

of the land would have been worse if the Maya had had cows and other stock to feed, as the modern settlers do.

The Lacandon forest, for all its vastness, is frail and vulnerable. The delicate balance of its life can too easily be upset by thoughtless felling and clearing away of trees.

The tropical soil is neither as deep nor as fertile as the earth of cooler lands. The ancient Maya were careful to build their cities in the river valleys where the soil is best for farming. The Lacandons also settle in the valleys and leave the forest cover on the steep, stony ridges. Even when clearing the land for their milpas, they spare the trees that are useful to them—the mahogany for its timber or the sweet zapote for its good fruit.

Where the forest stands undisturbed, the falling leaves build up a layer of leaf mold on the earth, just enough to nourish the trees and to create a constant cycle of growth and death and renewed fertility. When trees are cut down and the ground laid bare, the richness of the soil is quickly lost. The scorching sun

The way to a new home is long and hard for the Tzeltal pioneers.

57

destroys the layer of leaf mold, and lashing rain storms wash away the topsoil until the stones stick out of the earth like flesh-less bones.

The mighty trees themselves, dependent on the rains, help to make the climate of the rain forest. The moisture their roots receive from the saturated soil is given off by the leaves as water vapor, and a blanket of warm, damp air is spread over the tree-tops. Stripping the land of trees may reduce the quantity of life-giving rain.

Thus the climate and all forms of life in the forest are meshed together. Each living thing has its place in the ordered pattern, from the leaf-cutter ants that scurry along their clean-swept trails on the forest floor to the howler monkeys and par-rots in the treetops. Nothing is wasted. A giant tree is blown down in a summer storm and in a few months its fallen trunk has become a garden of ferns and orchids, sheltering a myriad population of insects and amphibians.

The Lacandon forest is only one of many places in the world where the balance of nature, once destroyed, cannot easily be restored. But here not only the life of animals and plants is endangered. Also at stake is the life of men.

The land that belonged to the ancient Maya, and where their ruined temples proclaim the glories of the past, is the birth-right of the Lacandons. The people of Nahá and Lacanhá are as much a part of the forest pattern as the trees and birds and deer; but their ties to the land are even deeper and stronger than the need for food and shelter. The forest has been for centuries their spiritual home, the place of their gods, made holy by long tradition. The land has nourished them in body and soul.

Yet the Lacandons have never owned the forest, as white men think of ownership. They have always moved about freely, settled where they pleased and used the riches of the forest ac-cording to their need. They were defenseless against the invasion of new settlers and exploiters of the land. They had no voice to

The stillness of Lake Nahá

*A young girl
of Nahá*

assert their right to live in peace in the home of their ancestors, and as their numbers dwindled, the Lacandons faced a future as dark and hopeless as the words of the old Maya prophecy.

Now at last all this is to be changed. Friends of the Indians have taken action to protect the land and the people.

The forest is to be saved from further destruction. The days of haphazard settlement and ruthless clearing are gone. New ways will be found to cut timber and to grow crops without leaving a trail of scarred, eroded earth, muddy streams, and polluted lakes. Roads will be built and villages planned for new settlers, but there will also be parks in the forest to preserve forever the Maya ruins, the blue waters, and the places of quiet green beauty. Above all, the lands where the Lacandons live will be theirs to possess for as long as they wish, undisturbed by invaders from outside.

Chank'in and his people, and those of Lacanhá, are to be owners of their land, their possession assured and their rights respected. The future holds life and hope for the Lacandons. But it will be a new kind of life. The whole forest will no longer be open to them for hunting, fishing, and farming. Inevitably their ways of living will be changed.

No one can tell how many of the Lacandons will choose to stay in the forest in the years to come. As roads are built and settlers arrive, the Lacandons will not be cut off from the outside world, a people set apart. Much will be gained by this, but some things, once precious, will be lost. With the passing of the older men, the old beliefs and traditions may die and ancient customs sink into oblivion. Even the discarding of traditional dress can be the sign of a change of heart.

Some of the young people, given new opportunities for schooling, will be eager to leave home and learn to work for wages in the white men's towns. A few of the Lacandons have already visited the world beyond the forest. Some wanted to stay

Young Chank'in, who can read and write Spanish, introduces Bor to the mystery of the written words.

61

there, but for others the ties with their own land and their own people were too strong to be broken.

Here in the forest, even today, the Lacandons can still enjoy some of the freedom for which their forefathers fought so hard. Each man is his own master. He thinks for himself, with no one to tell him how to act or what to believe. Yet independent as he is, he usually lives at peace with his neighbors. He respects the property of others and will not take what is not his, even in time of need. He will accept help and gifts from outsiders, especially food and medicines, but he will give something in return—the fruit of his fields, the work of his hands, or the sharing of his knowledge.

Old Chank'in and his people have given us much during our days with them in the forest. On the morning of our departure we remember the men and boys of Nahá paying their last visit to our camp. The forest was quiet in the heat of the afternoon, and no breeze stirred the lianas that hung from the crowns of the great trees. The Lacandons slipped silently into the camp in single file, coming from the narrow trail where Chank'in had once sung for us the Song of the Jaguar. They brought with them the bundle of flint-tipped arrows and the new mahogany table, trimmed to perfection. K'ayyum, the boy whose name means "Singing God," had something for us too, carefully stowed away in a bag.

After the talking and the laughter and the smoking of a fat homemade cigar, it was time for the men and boys to leave for home. Led by Old Chank'in, they departed as quietly as they had come. Good-byes were short, for in their own language the words of parting have no sorrow in them, only an acceptance of what must be.

"*Bin in ká*," says the one who goes away. "I go."

"*Shén!*" is the reply. "Go!"

This morning it is our turn to go. Our bags and bundles are stacked in the dew-wet grass, and while we wait for the coming

of the plane, K'in helps us to pick armfuls of flowers beside the green airstrip. Now we hear a sound in the sky fainter than the whir of the hummingbirds in the bushes. The plane appears high above and circles down to the lake. The noise swells to a grating roar as the plane skims low over the water and comes in to land.

Our bags and the bunches of flowers are quickly loaded and

The men and boys of Nahá go home through the forest.

we clamber aboard. K'in and one or two Lacandons from the houses near the airstrip stand quietly to watch us go.

The plane bumps and jolts to the end of the clearing, turns slowly, and comes roaring back. As it rises over the calm blue water of the lake, we have a last glimpse of the settlement on the far side and of the channels and lagoons of water lilies that we explored in the canoe. Then we are soaring over the carpet of the forest, casting our small shadow on treetops of a hundred shades of green, with here and there a tree in blossom or a little lake like a round blue eye.

Wedged carefully in a corner, on the floor of the plane, is a box containing the gift from K'ayyum. He has collected for us his finest clay jaguars, freshly painted in white, black, and yellow and wrapped for the journey in dry corn husks.

K'ayyum's offering seems to stand as a symbol of the world of the Lacandons and of their ancestors, the ancient Maya. Here are the corn and the jaguar, the milpa and the forest, the god of the growing maize and the god of darkness and the night. Once again the past and present are mingled in one flow of time. . . .

We have seen the Lacandons as links with the past, but they are far more than ghosts or shadows of their glorious ancestors. They are people who have learned to live in tune with their world, fighting only against those who have tried to rob them of their freedom. They have suffered hardship and tragedy, but they still know how to laugh. Their life has the beauty of simple things that can outlast the rise and fall of cities, and there is wisdom in the way of the people. When we are with them in the forest, we the outsiders are the primitive ones, clumsy and ignorant and with much to learn.

Now, as we look down from the sky at their good green land, we hear again the voice of Old Chank'in singing for us in the shade of the trees; and we remember the skillful hands of K'ayyum as he molded the figure of the jaguar, the lord of the forest and the gift of the Singing God.

DATE DUE

GAYLORD   PRINTED IN U.S.A.